WELCOME TO THE WHOLE WORLD OF
Elephants

Diane Swanson

Whitecap Books

Copyright © 2003 by Diane Swanson
Whitecap Books

Edited by Elizabeth McLean
Cover design by Steve Penner
Interior design by Margaret Ng
Typeset by Jacqui Thomas
Cover photograph by Thomas Kitchin
Photo credits: Thomas Kitchin iv, 8, 10, 16, 22; Wayne Lynch 2, 4, 6, 18;
Wendy Dennis/Dembinsky Photo Assoc 12, 16; Anup Shah/Dembinsky Photo Assoc 14, 24;
Stan Osolinski/Dembinsky Photo Assoc 20

Printed and bound in Hong Kong

National Library of Canada Cataloguing in Publication Data

Swanson, Diane, 1944–
    Welcome to the whole world of elephants/Diane Swanson.

    Includes index.
    ISBN 1-55285-451-5

    1. Elephants—Juvenile literature. I. Title.
QL737.P98S92 2003   j599.67   C2002-9111409-8

For more information on
this series and other
Whitecap Books titles,
visit our web site at
www.whitecap.ca

The publisher acknowledges the support of the Canada Council for the Arts and the Cultural
Services Branch of the Government of British Columbia for our publishing program. We
acknowledge the financial support of the Government of Canada through the Book Industry
Development Program for our publishing activities.

Contents

World of Difference

ELEPHANTS ARE ENORMOUS—the biggest land animals on Earth! African elephants are the tallest and heaviest. The males stand up to 4 metres (13 feet) high at the shoulder and can each weigh more than six small cars—6 tonnes (7 tons). Asian elephants are shorter and lighter, but they're still GIANTS among animals.

Both kinds of elephants sport long, snaky trunks—their noses and top lips, combined. Trunks are used mostly for breathing, smelling, feeling, and grabbing things, such as food. At the tip of its trunk, an African elephant has two fingerlike parts; an Asian

An African elephant has especially large ears.

1

Two bulges mark the forehead of an Asian elephant.

elephant has one. These nimble "fingers" can pick up objects as small as berries.

Male and female African elephants have huge pointed teeth, called tusks, that stick right out of their mouths. The sharp tusks make good weapons for fighting, but more often, they're tools for digging and scraping. Elephants usually favor either their right or their left tusk, just as people prefer using one hand over the other. But most female—and many male—Asian elephants have no tusks at all.

Elephants see better in shadows than in bright light, but they depend more on their strong senses of smell and touch to explore their world. They hear quite well, too, and they also use their big, floppy ears to help threaten their enemies. Held out to the sides, the ears make elephants look even larger than usual.

Elephants amaze people. Here are some of the reasons why:

 Underwater, elephants can use their trunks like snorkels to breathe.

 Tusks never stop growing. One of the longest tusks on an African elephant measured about 3.5 metres (11 feet).

 A tall elephant may hold out one of its ears to shade a shorter elephant from the sun.

 Elephants can find distant watering holes, even ones they haven't visited for months.

Where in the World

LUSH, GREEN FORESTS AND DRY, BROWN GRASSLANDS—both make homes for elephants. Some of the animals live on cool, rugged mountains; others on hot, flat plains. But they seldom wander far from streams or lakes.

Each kind of elephant is named for the continent it's found on. African elephants live in parts of Africa south of the Sahara Desert. Asian elephants live in parts of southern Asia, including India.

Wherever they roam, elephants need plenty of space. As big beasts, they have to travel far and wide to find enough food.

Roving the range, an elephant grazes as it goes.

5

The shady jungle helps keep an elephant cool.

Grown males ramble around alone or, occasionally, with a few other males. But female elephants walk their world together. They move as families of sisters, daughters, aunts, and nieces—along with all their newborns and calves that are less than 10 or 12 years old. A family group is usually led by its eldest female. She is also likely to be the largest in the family because elephants never stop growing.

When a family of elephants is on the move, it often meets up with other families. Then they all might travel together for a while as a herd.

Stopping for naps night and day, elephants first search for sheltered sleeping places. They might lie down, some-times gathering soft plants to form pillows beneath their heavy heads. But they frequently sleep standing up, resting their trunks on the ground.

Wild elephants today live in warm climates, but that wasn't always the case. Of the 500 different kinds of elephants that have roamed Earth during the last several million years, some were well adapted to cold climates.

Ancient elephants called woolly mammoths even survived in North America and in the far north of Siberia, Russia. Thick layers of fat and dense hairy coats kept them warm. And the mammoths dug through snow with their curved tusks to reach grass.

World Full of Food

Standing tall, an elephant stretches to snatch leaves from a tree.

EATING IS A FULL-TIME JOB—for an elephant. To support its gigantic body, it needs many meals every day. In just 24 hours, an adult elephant can eat food that weighs as much as 800 to 1300 hamburgers!

During the wet seasons in Africa and Asia, elephants graze on grass, grabbing big bunches with their trunks. They might beat the grass against their front legs to shake dirt off the roots before eating. In the dry seasons, elephants browse trees, using their trunks to pluck leaves and twigs. Sometimes an elephant stands only on its back legs so its trunk can reach leaves high up.

9

Elephants also dine on fruit and seedpods, which they pick or shake from trees. They often wade into lakes and swamps to stuff themselves with water plants. And they add a daily drink to their meals by sucking up water with their trunks. Then they tilt their heads back, stick the tips of

With a bite of lunch curled tightly in its trunk, an elephant feeds.

the trunks inside their mouths, and let the water flow.

Elephants use their trunks to put food right into their mouths. In a minute, they can gather, cram, and eat nine or ten trunkfuls of grass. Four huge teeth—each one longer than this page—grind up every bite.

As an elephant's chewing teeth wear down or fall out, they are replaced several times. When the last set is completely worn—usually in 50 to 70 years—the elephants can no longer chew, and they die.

UNDERGROUND ELEPHANTS

Just like people, elephants need a little salt in their diets. Along the border between Kenya and Uganda, African elephants file into a mountain cave to "mine" for salt.

The elephants use their trunks to feel their way through the deep, dark cave. When they find some salt rocks, they chip them out with their tusks. The animals visit the mountain cave almost nightly, earning the nickname "underground elephants."

11

World of Words

ELEPHANTS HAVE TRUNKS THAT TALK. A calf hooks its long nose around its mother's back leg to say, "Wait!" An adult slaps its trunk on a calf to say it's time to settle down. Trunks are also used to hug and pat family members. The animals might flap their ears as well, which strengthens the message: "I like you."

Like many other animals, elephants talk through sounds, too. They trumpet loudly with their trunks, announcing they are angry or excited. Young calves growl to let their mothers know they're hungry, and they scream to demand attention. Adults

One elephant pats another in a friendly "hello."

13

Whine, growl. A calf presses its mother for another meal.

sometimes bark at older calves, warning them not to wander off.

But a lot of elephant talk is neither seen nor heard—by people, that is. Many of the animal's sounds are too low-pitched to be picked up by human ears. Trees and grass don't block these rumblings as much as they do high-pitched sounds, such as whistles.

That means elephants can send low-pitched messages to other elephants more than 4 kilometres (2.5 miles) away. As well, these messages make the ground vibrate, which sends the signals even farther.

All this long-distance chatter is important for animals that travel around as much as elephants do. It helps males and females find one another when they are ready to mate. And it might warn families of danger or tell them the locations of watering holes.

Elephants not only understand "elephant talk," they can also learn to understand people. Human trainers are able to teach the animals to follow about 100 different commands, such as kneel, stand, go, turn, stop, and lift. The elephants can also learn new skills from trainers, including sitting down—something they don't do naturally—and untying knots.

Trained elephants are used to carry people, entertain crowds with tricks, and do heavy work, like lifting and hauling logs.

New World

WHEN THEY'RE ONLY AN HOUR OLD, ELEPHANTS CAN WALK—even keep up with their family. But the newborns move stiffly and trip easily. They often step on their own trunks and fall down. Then they cry—noisy, squeaky screams—for attention.

It doesn't take a young elephant long to start exploring. From its first day, a newborn uses its trunk to smell, feel, and tug whatever's around. Soon it tries to lift things, too. But sometimes the little calf takes time out to suck the tip of its trunk, much like a human baby sucks a thumb.

When there's nothing much to do, a calf can always suck its trunk.

17

Asian elephants watch protectively over a young calf.

A calf spends most of its first few months close to its mother. She pats and strokes the calf as it leans against her. Frequently, the calf stays right beneath her belly as they walk. And when they nap, it usually lays its head on her body.

At first, the calf feeds only on its mother's milk, but soon it starts nibbling grass and leaves as well. It also learns to drink water, kneeling at first to sip with its mouth before trying to draw the water up its trunk.

Mother elephants get plenty of help raising their calves. Other females and older calves keep a close eye on any newborn. They try to make sure it doesn't wander off, but if it does, they are quick to bring it back.

Lions in Africa and tigers in Asia might attack a young elephant. If they threaten a calf, the older elephants in the family form a protective circle around it.

Being born into a family with an elderly leader helps an elephant calf grow strong and stay safe. An old elephant can draw on many memories of searching for food and water. And she can usually find the best places for her family to eat and drink.

The elderly elephant also remembers the calls of many of the elephants she meets, so she can sort friends from strangers. Then the family can act to protect its calves from unfriendly elephants.

Small World

ELEPHANT CALVES HAVE A LOT TO LEARN. Even eating takes practice. One of the hardest skills a calf has to master is feeding on short grass. The calf tries to wind its trunk around a single blade—something that calls for several patient attempts. When the calf breaks off the blade, it is likely to drop the grass. Then the elephant struggles, again and again, to pick it up.

When hunger makes a calf too impatient to try to feed with its trunk, it might drop down on its knees and simply bite off the grass. Or it might snatch bits of food as they fall from the mouths of bigger

Sneaking close, a calf steals food right from an elephant's mouth.

21

Ah! There's nothing like a mud bath to make a calf feel frisky.

elephants. Some calves try to yank grass and leaves right out of the munching mouths of others.

Calves must learn to groom themselves. They shower and bathe, rolling around in shallow water. Then they use their trunks to suck up dust or mud and spray their bodies. The layer of dirt helps get rid of pests and protects the elephants from the strong sun.

A calf soon discovers it can relieve itches by scratching with the tip of its trunk or by rubbing itself against trees. For hard-to-reach places, such as the belly, it figures out how to hold a stick with its trunk and scratch.

As a calf gets older, its mother lets other family members answer its cries more often. Then she has time to look after herself and, perhaps, a new calf. Elephants are often born four years apart.

THICK AND WRINKLY

As a young elephant matures, its skin grows thicker. Parts of its hide become four times as thick as human skin. Still, the hide is sensitive. Elephants, like people, can sunburn and sense insect bites.

Having wrinkled skin is good for an elephant. The deep creases hold moisture, which cools the animal, and they help make each elephant different. The pattern of wrinkles on its lower legs are unique in every individual.

23

Fun World

BIG ELEPHANTS, LITTLE ELEPHANTS—ALL ELEPHANTS PLAY. And when elephants of different sizes play together, the taller ones make themselves "shorter" by kneeling or lying down.

Elephant calves spend the greatest amount of time at play. One of their most popular games is climbing on large elephants that are lying on the grass. The calves also stretch out together, especially wherever there's mud. Then they scramble and slide over one another's slippery bodies.

Many elephant games involve running. One animal might chase after another and

Two playmates take part in a wild elephant game.

25

Young elephants enjoy some clean, wet fun together.

try to grab it by the tail. Or two elephants might pretend to charge. They trumpet loudly and gallop toward each other. Sometimes elephants butt heads or play-fight by pushing and shoving or by wrestling with their trunks.

Water play is fun for elephants. They like to splash and make waves. Best of all, they suck water up their trunks and spray it at their playmates.

Elephant toys are whatever elephants find. Calves toss leaves into the air, then dash through them. Adults fling small trees. Elephants even attack logs, stomping and kicking them until they break.

With their families close by for safety, young calves might spend 10 minutes playing before they're all worn out. But the games of older calves and adult elephants can last more than an hour.

BUFFALO PLAYMATES

A male elephant calf on an African plain is hiding in tall grass. Only a few months old, he is ready and eager for fun. Usually he plays with other elephants in his family. But today, he can't resist teasing some cape buffalo calves.

As a herd of cape buffalo wanders by, the little elephant suddenly bursts out of the grass, startling one of the calves. Then he returns to his hiding spot until the next calf appears—and charges out again.

Index